The
Book of Hearts

The
Book of Hearts

Visions of Love,
in Word and Image

Running Press
Philadelphia • London

Library of Congress Cataloging-in-Publication Number
93–87407

ISBN 1–56138–416–X

This book may be ordered by mail from the publisher. Please
add $1.00 for postage and handling. *But try your bookstore first!*

Running Press Book Publishers
125 South Twenty-second Street
Philadelphia, Pennsylvania 19103–4399

Contents

Introduction

Love could not have a more per-
fect symbol than the heart — a shape
composed of two gracefully curving
lines, symmetrical and joined, like
lovers who reflect each other and
form two halves of a greater whole.
The Book of Hearts gathers these
symbols of love. Here are profound
words of wonder and devotion, illus-
trated with works of power, wit, and

beauty by some of this century's great artists.

Find yourself in these explorations, and share them with someone you love.

From the
Heart

Go to your bosom;

Knock there, and ask your heart

what it doth know.

— WILLIAM SHAKESPEARE (1564–1616)
ENGLISH DRAMATIST AND POET

THE HEART IS LIKE AN INSTRUMENT
WHOSE STRINGS STEAL NOBLER MUSIC
FROM LIFE'S MANY FRETS.

— *GERALD MASSEY (1828–1907)*
ENGLISH POET

Only where the heart is
can the treasure be found.

—*JAMES BARRIE (1860–1937)*
SCOTTISH NOVELIST AND
DRAMATIST

CAROL SUMMERS
Pool

The openhearted and open-minded

people are the strong ones. . . .

They have the most power because

they give instead of take. They give and

gain while the takers lose.

—SUSAN TROTT (B. 1937)
AMERICAN WRITER

THE HEART OUTSTRIPS THE CLUMSY SENSES, AND SEES — PERHAPS FOR AN INSTANT, PERHAPS FOR LONG PERIODS OF BLISS — AN UNDISTORTED AND MORE VERITABLE WORLD.

—*EVELYN UNDERHILL (1875–1941)*
ENGLISH MYSTIC

It is only with the heart
that one can see rightly;
what is essential is
invisible to the eye.

—*ANTOINE DE SAINT-EXUPÉRY*
(1900–1944)
FRENCH WRITER AND AVIATOR

Love is space and time made directly

perceptible to the heart.

—*MARCEL PROUST (1871–1922)*
FRENCH NOVELIST

T. YOKOI
Tulip

. . . IF THERE WAS SUCH A THING AS IMMORTALITY, LOVE WAS PROBABLY AT ITS HEART.

—*NORMAN GARBO (B. 1919)*
AMERICAN WRITER

KEITH HARING
Untitled

I am certain of nothing but
of the holiness of the
Heart's affections and the
truth of Imagination —
What the imagination
seizes as Beauty must
be truth. . .

—*JOHN KEATS (1795–1821)*
ENGLISH POET

. . . each action taken in this world has

its echo in the heart.

— *GELSEY KIRKLAND (B. 1952)*
AMERICAN BALLERINA

If you haven't had at least
a slight poetic crack in the
heart, you have been
cheated by nature.

—*PHYLLIS BATTELLE (B. 1922)*
AMERICAN JOURNALIST

My heart was full to overflowing with

an emotion I didn't understand then, or

believe it was necessary to understand,

not old or wise enough to know that

there's a magic in the moonlight of every

parting that can't survive the bright

light of real life.

—*DAVID PAYNE (B. 1951)*
AMERICAN WRITER

HE WAS STILL TOO YOUNG TO KNOW
THAT THE HEART'S MEMORY ELIMI-
NATES THE BAD AND MAGNIFIES THE
GOOD, AND THAT THANKS TO THIS
ARTIFICE WE MANAGE TO ENDURE
THE BURDEN OF THE PAST.

—*GABRIEL GARCÍA MÁRQUEZ (B. 1928)*
COLOMBIAN WRITER

That is where the golden knowledge is, the important parts, signs of danger, of safety, of what is within the secret heart. Remember, all of us here, men and women, have three hearts, one for all the world to see, one for their family, and one for themselves alone.

—JAMES CLAVELL (B. 1925)
AUSTRALIAN-BORN AMERICAN
WRITER

All the knowledge I possess everyone else

can acquire, but my heart is

all my own.

— JOHANN WOLFGANG VON GOETHE
(1749–1832)
GERMAN POET

JOSEPH CORNELL
Untitled *(Tamara Toumanova in "Moonlight Sonata")*
© The Joseph and Robert Cornell Memorial Foundation

The heart of man is made to reconcile

contradictions.

—DAVID HUME (1711–1776)
SCOTTISH PHILOSOPHER AND HISTORIAN

ALL GREAT DISCOVERIES WERE MADE
BY MEN WHOSE FEELINGS RUN AHEAD
OF THEIR THINKING.

—*CHARLES HENRY PARKHURST (1842–1933)*
AMERICAN CLERGYMAN

The heart has arguments with which

the understanding is not acquainted.

— *RALPH WALDO EMERSON (1803–1882)*
AMERICAN ESSAYIST AND POET

PAUL KLEE
Love Song during the New Moon

TO LOVE IS TO ADMIRE WITH THE
HEART; TO ADMIRE IS TO LOVE WITH
THE MIND.

— *THÉOPHILE GAUTIER (1811–1872)*
FRENCH MAN OF LETTERS

The head never rules the heart, but just becomes its partner in crime.

—*MIGNON MCLAUGHLIN*
AMERICAN WRITER

The wrinkles of the heart are more

indelible than those of the brow.

—MADAME DOROTHÉE DELUZY (1747–1830)
FRENCH ACTRESS

. . . WE KNOW THINGS BETTER
THROUGH LOVE THAN THROUGH
KNOWLEDGE.

— UMBERTO ECO (B. 1932)
ITALIAN SCHOLAR AND NOVELIST

MAN HAS MADE MANY MACHINES,
COMPLEX AND CUNNING, BUT WHICH
OF THEM INDEED RIVALS THE WORK-
ING OF HIS HEART?

—*PABLO CASALS (1876–1973)*
SPANISH VIOLINCELLIST AND CONDUCTOR

The heart is a free and
fetterless thing—
A wave of the ocean,
a bird on the wing.

—*JULIA PARDOE (1806–1862)*
ENGLISH WRITER

In each human heart are a tiger, a pig,

an ass and a nightingale.

Diversity of character is due to their

unequal activity.

—*AMBROSE BIERCE (1842–?1914)*
AMERICAN JOURNALIST AND WRITER

KURT SCHWITTERS
Aquarell no. 1.
The Heart Goes from Sugar to Coffee, 1919

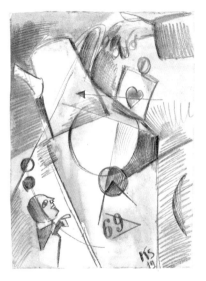

ADORNMENT IS NEVER ANYTHING
EXCEPT A REFLECTION OF THE HEART.

— *Coco Chanel (1883–1970)*
French fashion designer

All that is in the heart is
written in the face.

—*AFRICAN PROVERB*

Hearts have as many fashions as the

world has shapes.

—OVID (43 B.C.–?17 A.D.)
ROMAN POET

I DON'T KNOW WHAT IS BETTER THAN THE WORK THAT IS GIVEN TO THE ACTOR — TO TEACH THE HUMAN HEART THE KNOWLEDGE OF ITSELF.

— *SIR LAURENCE OLIVIER (1907–1989)*
ENGLISH ACTOR

In a series of kindnesses
there is at last one which
makes the heart run over.

—*James Boswell (1740–1795)*
Scottish lawyer and man of
letters

The human heart is unsearchable.

Who is to fathom it?

— *WILKIE COLLINS (1824–1889)*
ENGLISH NOVELIST

II

Losing Your Heart

THE HEART OF A MAN HAS BEEN COM-
PARED TO FLOWERS; BUT UNLIKE
THEM, IT DOES NOT WAIT FOR THE
BLOWING OF THE WIND TO BE SCAT-
TERED ABROAD.

— *Yohida Kenko*
13th–century Japanese poet

My heart is like fire in a closed vessel: I

am ready to burst for want of vent.

—JOHN WESLEY (1703–1791)
ENGLISH RELIGIOUS LEADER

The heart is forever
inexperienced.

—*HENRY DAVID THOREAU*
(1817–1862)
AMERICAN WRITER AND
NATURALIST

WHEN A YOUNG MAN COMPLAINS
THAT A YOUNG LADY HAS NO HEART,
IT IS A PRETTY CERTAIN SIGN THAT
SHE HAS HIS.

—*GEORGE D. PRENTICE (1802–1870)*
AMERICAN JOURNALIST

"Intrusions?" He had
smiled the word away.
"You can't well intrude,
my darling, on a heart
where you've already
established yourself to the
complete exclusion of
other lodgers."

—EDITH WHARTON (1862–1937)
AMERICAN NOVELIST

MARCEL DUCHAMP
Fluttering Hearts from "Boite-en-Valise"

THE VERIE INSTANT THAT I SAW
YOU, DID
MY HEART FLIE TO YOUR SERVICE.

— *WILLIAM SHAKESPEARE (1564–1616)*
ENGLISH DRAMATIST AND POET

My heart is a desert island,

and she lives in it alone.

—CHARLES DICKENS (1812–1870)
ENGLISH NOVELIST

What can the will do when
the heart commands?

—LOUIS L'AMOUR (1908–1988)
AMERICAN NOVELIST

BYRON BRATT
Language of the Heart

If it had gone to thee, I know

Mine would have taught thy

heart to show

More pity unto me: but Love, alas,

At one first blow did shiver it as glass.

—JOHN DONNE (1572–1631)
ENGLISH POET

It is better to break one's
heart than to do nothing
with it.

—*MARGARET KENNEDY*
(1896–1967)
ENGLISH WRITER

THE HUMAN HEART IS LIKE INDIAN
RUBBER: A LITTLE SWELLS IT, BUT A
GREAT DEAL WILL NOT BURST IT.

—*ANNE BRONTË (1820–1849)*
ENGLISH NOVELIST

ARSHILE GORKY
Valentine

Everything is as
problematic as geometry
when it's affairs of the
heart in question.

—*RICHARD FORD (B. 1944)*
AMERICAN WRITER

JAMES RIZZI
Love is in the Air

HEARTS LIVE BY BEING WOUNDED.

—*OSCAR WILDE (1854–1900)*
IRISH POET AND PLAYWRIGHT

YOU KNOW, A HEART CAN BE BROKEN, BUT IT KEEPS ON BEATING, JUST THE SAME.

—*FANNIE FLAGG (B. 1941)*
AMERICAN ACTRESS AND NOVELIST

A broken heart is what makes life so

wonderful five years later,

when you see the guy in an elevator

and he is fat and smoking a cigar and

saying long-time-no-see.

—PHYLLIS BATTELLE (B. 1922)
AMERICAN JOURNALIST

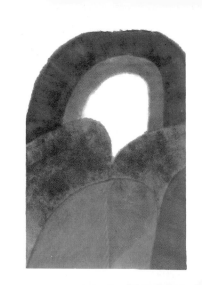

Always there remain
portions of our heart into
which no one is able to
enter, invite them as
we may.

—MARY DIXON THAYER (B. 1896)
AMERICAN POET

CAROL SUMMERS
Ryder's Evening

DAILY THE BODY CHANGES, DAILY
THE MIND—WHY NOT THE HEART?

—*GEORGE MEREDITH (1828–1909)*
ENGLISH NOVELIST AND POET

. . . my heart does not wish to be in a

mending situation. Love is

heart-breaking and I am in love!

—RACHEL BILLINGTON (B. 1942)
ENGLISH WRITER

The human heart, at
whatever age, opens only
to the heart that opens
in return.

—*MARIA EDGEWORTH*
(1767–1849)
BRITISH WRITER

WE LOVE BEING IN LOVE, THAT'S THE TRUTH ON'T.

— *WILLIAM MAKEPEACE THACKERAY*
(1811–1863)
ENGLISH NOVELIST

III

Heart to Heart

Alas, that my heart is a lute,
Whereon you have learned to play!
For many years it was mute,
Until one summer's day
You took it, and touched it, and
made it thrill
And it thrills and throbs,
and quivers still!

—ANNE LINDSAY (1750–1825)
ENGLISH POET

SOMETIMES A COMING TOGETHER IS POSSIBLE, A SPILLING OF ONE REALITY INTO ANOTHER. A KIND OF SOFT ENLACING. . . . JUST . . . WELL . . . BREATHING. YES, THAT'S THE SOUND OF IT. MAYBE THE FEEL OF IT, TOO. BREATHING.

—ROBERT JAMES WALLER (B. 1959)
AMERICAN WRITER AND PHOTOGRAPHER

What closeness! Only the
human animals join so
close: heart to heart,
mouth to mouth. See how
that sets us and it apart so
that it isn't only sex. . .

—*SUSAN TROTT* (B. 1937)
AMERICAN WRITER

HENRI MATISSE
"Icarus" from Jazz

You gave me the key to your

heart my love,

Then why did you make me knock?

—*GEORGE GORDON, LORD BYRON*
(1788–1824)
ENGLISH POET

A HEART IS A LOCK, BUT A LOCK CAN
BE OPENED WITH A DUPLICATE KEY.

— *YIDDISH PROVERB*

My heart shall be thy
garden.

—*Alice Meynell (1847–1922)*
English poet

CAROL SUMMERS
Memory

But we will have a way more liberal,

Than changing hearts, to join them,

so we shall

Be one, and one another's all.

—JOHN DONNE (1572–1631)
ENGLISH POET

ONE TURF SHALL SERVE AS PILLOW
FOR US BOTH;
ONE HEART, ONE BED, TWO BOSOMS
AND ONE TROTH.

— *WILLIAM SHAKESPEARE (1564–1616)*
ENGLISH DRAMATIST AND POET

Love does not consist in
gazing at each other but in
looking outward together
in the same direction.

—*ANTOINE DE SAINT-EXUPÉRY*
(1900–1944)
FRENCH WRITER AND AVIATOR

In that secret space of time, I will

kiss the inside of your smile.

Not with my mouth, but through

my heart, as we share a journey

to the stars.

— CHRISTINA CRAWFORD (B. 1939)
AMERICAN AUTHOR AND LECTURER

With All
Your Heart

There is a chord in every heart that has a sigh in it if touched aright.

—*MARIE LOUISE DE LA RAMÉE*
(1839–1908)
ENGLISH WRITER

ALL MY HEART IS YOURS, SIR: IT
BELONGS TO YOU; AND WITH YOU IT
WOULD REMAIN, WERE FATE TO EXILE
THE REST OF ME FROM YOUR PRES-
ENCE FOR EVER.

— *CHARLOTTE BRONTË (1816–1855)*
ENGLISH NOVELIST

Nothing exists that so fills and

binds the heart as love does.

— UMBERTO ECO (B. 1932)
ITALIAN SCHOLAR AND NOVELIST

LOVE IS OF ALL PASSIONS THE
STRONGEST, FOR IT ATTACKS SIMULTA-
NEOUSLY THE HEAD, THE HEART AND
THE SENSES.

— *VOLTAIRE (1694–1778)*
FRENCH WRITER

If we all take the time to look into our hearts, we will ultimately feel complete and connected . . . within ourselves and as part of the human family.

—*SUSAN JEFFERS*
AMERICAN PSYCHIATRIST AND WRITER

KEITH HARING
Untitled

THERE ARE NO LITTLE EVENTS WITH
THE HEART. IT MAGNIFIES EVERY-
THING; IT PLACES IN THE SAME
SCALES THE FALL OF AN EMPIRE OF
FOURTEEN YEARS AND THE DROPPING
OF A WOMAN'S GLOVE, AND ALMOST
ALWAYS THE GLOVE WEIGHS MORE
THAN THE EMPIRE.

—HONORÉ DE BALZAC (1799–1850)
FRENCH WRITER

Where heart, and soul, and sense,

in concert move,

And the blood's lava,

and the pulse a blaze,

Each kiss a heart-quake.

— GEORGE GORDON, LORD BYRON (1788–1824)
ENGLISH POET

Wear me as a seal upon

your heart

as a seal upon your arm;

for love is strong as

death. . .

— *SONG OF SONGS, 8:6*

JOAN MIRÓ
Danseuse II

WE SHOULD COUNT TIME BY HEART-
THROBS.

—*PHILIP JAMES BAILEY (1816–1902)*
ENGLISH POET

The emotions may be endless.

The more we express them, the more

we may have to express.

—*E.M. FORSTER (1879–1970)*
ENGLISH NOVELIST

Love was, to his

impassion'd soul,

Not, as with others, a

mere part

Of his existence, but the

whole,

The very life-breath of

his heart!

— *THOMAS MOORE (1779–1852)*
IRISH POET

YOU ARE MY SYMPATHY—MY BETTER SELF—MY GOOD ANGEL—I AM BOUND TO YOU WITH A STRONG ATTACHMENT. I THINK YOU GOOD, GIFTED, LOVELY: A FERVENT, A SOLEMN PASSION IS CONCEIVED IN MY HEART; IT LEANS TO YOU, DRAWS YOU TO MY CENTRE AND SPRING OF LIFE, WRAPS MY EXISTENCE ABOUT YOU— AND, KINDLING IN PURE, POWERFUL FLAME, FUSES YOU AND ME IN ONE.

—*CHARLOTTE BRONTË (1816–1855)*
ENGLISH NOVELIST

This book has been bound
using handcraft methods, and Smyth-sewn
to ensure durability.

The dust jacket was designed by Toby Schmidt.

The interior was designed by Christian Benton.

The art was researched by Elizabeth Broadrup.

The book was edited by Gregory C. Aaron.

The text was set in Cochin and
Adobe Garamond, with FC Ariston,
by Richard Conklin.